PENGUINS
BIRDS THAT SWIM

Written by Benjamin J. Pernick

Macmillan
McGraw-Hill
New York Farmington

It's hard to believe that penguins are birds. Instead of flying, they swim.

Penguins spend most of their life in the water. They come on land to lay eggs, hatch, and raise their chicks.

Most birds get food and escape from enemies by flying. But penguins get food from the sea. And adult penguins have very few enemies. So penguins can live without flying.

Most penguins live in the southern hemisphere and the Antarctic. But two kinds of penguins live near the equator. They live where there is food for them all year round.

A penguin's body helps to keep it warm and dry. Under its skin is a thick layer of fat. This layer keeps the penguin warm when it swims in cold water or walks on snow and ice.

A penguin has two layers of feathers. The feathers trap a layer of warm air around the penguin's body. The outer layer of feathers is waterproof. These features keep the penguin dry when it swims.

Adult penguins swim fast. Their flippers help them move and their flat feet help them steer. They can swim as fast as 20 miles an hour.

To breathe while they are swimming, penguins leap and skim over the water. Then they plunge back into the water. Because the penguin looks like a porpoise when it leaps across the water, this kind of swimming is called *porpoising*.

When a penguin wants to jump from water onto a high ice ridge, it starts building up speed while it is swimming. Then it shoots out of the water and lands feet first. When going back into the water to feed, a penguin jumps in belly first with a loud splash.

The penguin's greatest enemy is the leopard seal. It kills penguins for food. To catch a penguin, the seal swims near places where penguins go in and out of the water. Sometimes, the seal hides on land under an ice ridge and waits for a penguin to come close. The seals also try to catch penguins while they are swimming.

A large group of penguins will often gather at the edge of the water and wait until they feel it is safe to jump in. The bravest or hungriest one goes in first. If there are no enemies in the water, the others follow.

Some people think all penguins look alike. But there are seventeen kinds of penguins. And they don't all look alike.

The emperor penguin is the largest. It can grow to be 4 feet tall and weigh about 65 pounds. It has a smooth head and body. There is a strip of orange around its bill and on the back of its small neck. Its bill is long and pointed. The emperor has a thicker coat of feathers than other penguins. The emperor penguin's feet are black and its ankles have feathers around them that help keep them warm. Three claws on each foot help the emperor penguin move on the ice.

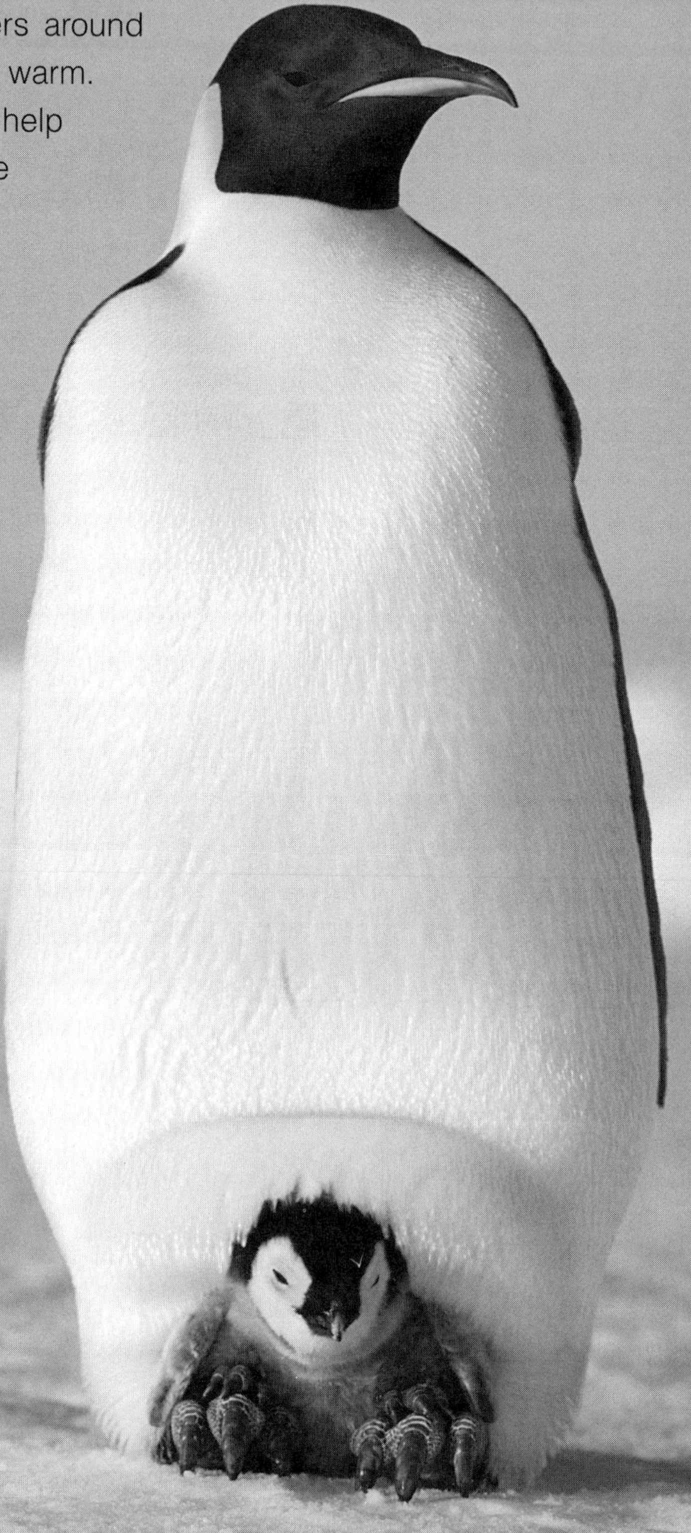

The rockhopper penguin is smaller. It has long gold feathers that stick out over its red eyes and tufts of short black feathers on top of its head. Its red or orange bill is shorter than the emperor penguin's bill. The rockhopper's feet are pink and have three sharp claws to help it climb rocks.

The little blue penguin is the smallest of all. It weighs about 2 to 3 pounds and is only about 15 inches tall. Its back feathers are dark blue. Its front feathers are white, as are the tip of its tail and the back of its flippers. Its bill is black, and there are black feathers around its yellow eyes.

The different kinds of penguins lay eggs and raise their chicks in different ways.

The emperor penguin is the only penguin that will lay an egg when the weather is freezing and the snow is blowing. When it is time for egg laying, the emperor penguins come out of the water, form a single line and follow a leader. They travel on ice for many miles to get away from the water.

These penguins don't use a nest. The male takes the egg from the female and tucks it into a fold of skin on its lower belly. The egg rests on the male's feet, where it stays safe and warm. The male keeps the egg this way, without eating, for two months. During this time the female goes off to feed. She comes back when the egg is ready to hatch.

Male emperor penguins huddle together to keep warm while they wait for their eggs to hatch. Some groups may have over a million penguins.

A short while after the chick is hatched, the parents go back to the sea to get food for the chick. While the parents are gone, the chicks huddle together to keep warm.

After the chick has grown, the adult penguins grow a new set of feathers. This is called molting. After molting, parents and chicks return to the sea.

Rockhoppers raise their chicks on islands north of the Antarctic. In the spring and summer, they ride on huge waves toward shore. They jump off when the waves break on the rocks.

Rockhoppers build their nests on top of high cliffs. They come back to the same nest year after year. To reach their nests, they climb up paths that rockhoppers have used for years. These paths have deep ridges in them that were made by penguins' claws. As the penguins climb, they jump from rock to rock. This is why they are called rockhoppers.

The rockhopper makes its nest out of mud. The birds use their feet to make a mound. Then they put some blades of grass on top.

Two eggs are laid. The first one is small and usually does not hatch. If it does hatch, the chick does not live very long.

The parents take turns feeding and protecting the chick that hatches from the second egg. They have to protect it from the Johnny Rook, a bird that tries to eat chicks.

The smallest penguin, the little blue, is sometimes called a fairy penguin. It lives on the coasts of New Zealand and on islands along the south coast of Australia.

The little blues spend the day in the water, safe from land animals and birds that would attack them. They feed on small fish. At night they come out of the water and go to their nests.

Their nests are burrows, small holes made in mud and shaded grassy areas. Small rocks in front of it protect the nest from enemies.

Little blue penguins lay two to three eggs and both parents care for the chicks. The chicks have many enemies, such as sea birds, falcons, eagles, snakes, and even rats. So the penguin parents need to keep a careful eye out for them.

Today, humans are the penguins' greatest enemy. Oil spills from ships have reached the Antarctic. When oil coats a penguin's feathers, the feathers no longer protect the penguin from the cold. If the bird tries to lick off the oil, it can be poisoned.

Fishermen are catching more and more fish in waters where penguins live. This is making it hard for penguins to find enough food.

Scientists all over the world are working to keep the penguins' habitat safe. They want penguins to be around for a long time.